AN EXCITING JOURNEY TOWARD YOUR DREAM HOME

F.A. Shahid

ARCHWAY
PUBLISHING

Archway Publishing books may be ordered through booksellers or by contacting:

Archway Publishing
1663 Liberty Drive
Bloomington, IN 47403
www.archwaypublishing.com
1 (888) 242-5904

Because of the dynamic nature of the Internet, any web addresses or
links contained in this book may have changed since publication and
may no longer be valid. The views expressed in this work are solely those
of the author and do not necessarily reflect the views of the publisher,
and the publisher hereby disclaims any responsibility for them.

Any people depicted in stock imagery provided by Thinkstock are models,
and such images are being used for illustrative purposes only.
Certain stock imagery © Thinkstock.

ISBN: 978-1-4808-1953-5 (sc)
ISBN: 978-1-4808-1954-2 (e)

Library of Congress Control Number: 2015946802

Print information available on the last page.

Archway Publishing rev. date: 10/28/2015

This book is dedicated to my mother, who always advised me to show generosity and benevolence toward my fellow beings.

In addition, I dedicate this book to my loving wife, who always trusts me, assists me and provides me excellent consultation in all of my important endeavours.

CONTENTS

FOREWORD

I connected with Fazal Shahid at a Real Estate Brokerage, *Century 21 People's Choice*, in Toronto a few years ago when he expressed his willingness to sponsor our bi-weekly newspaper, *Akhbar-e-Jahan Toronto*. During the course of our connection, I found Mr. Shahid to be an honest, sincere and helpful person. Later on, I came to know that he was an experienced realtor. I requested him to write some articles on various topics involving real estate for the benefit of our readers, especially first-time homebuyers.

At first I thought Mr. Shahid, as a very busy realtor, would find it hard to spare the time to write these articles. I was surprised and delighted when he called and informed me that he had emailed me the first episode in the series of his real estate articles, titled "An Exciting Journey." He continued to write many more articles, which we published in our newspaper. The articles were very easy to understand, interesting, well-explained and beneficial for our readers. His series of articles became very popular for our readers, homebuyers, home sellers and even other realtors.

Now, Fazal Shahid has decided to publish these articles in the form of a book, *An Exciting Journey Toward Your Dream Home*. I am ecstatic to congratulate him for his wonderful efforts on publishing this book. I am sure this book will be a useful, practical and beneficial asset to the world of real estate.

Azfar Jamil, Realtor
Editor, *Akhbar-e-Jahan Toronto*
November 25, 2014

PREFACE

Last year, I received a phone call from a gentleman in response to my advertisement in the local newspaper, *Akhbar-e-Jahan, Toronto*. He mentioned he came to Canada two years ago and was renting an apartment for $1,500 per month. He inquired thoroughly regarding the opportunity to buy a home in Canada. This led me to think about all the new immigrants who come to Canada every year. Surely, they need guidance and relevant information to help them in the process of buying a home. With this in mind, I decided to write some articles on the subject and ultimately publish this book.

An Exciting Journey Toward Your Dream Home is addressed to the public to provide general information for those who have visions of owning their dream home, but fear to take the necessary steps to make this vision a reality.

Then, I also thought of the homeowners who are in the process of selling their home. They also need appropriate guidance in the selling process to achieve the best possible value for their home. This led me to my explanation of real estate investment from an investor's point of view.

I hope and pray that my humble efforts in writing this book will be beneficial and helpful for all readers, specifically first-time home-buyers, existing homeowners and real estate investors.

ACKNOWLEDGEMENTS

This book could not have been completed without the assistance of many people. I would like to sincerely thank Mr. Azfar Jamil for the valuable suggestions, encouragement and appreciation, which gave me the inspiration and strength to write this book. I greatly appreciate and thank Usman Shahid who spent significant time and effort for the final reviewing. I also thank Hassaan Shahid and Hibba-tul-Noor Nasir for their constant assistance during the process of writing this book. Moreover, I cannot forget the encouragement I got from my friends and colleagues, to whom I am very thankful. A special thanks also to Maham Shahid-Aziz and Soniya Ahmed, who always provided me with assistance and contributed insightful ideas during the process of publishing this book.

CHAPTER 1

WHY SHOULD WE BUY A HOME?

INTRODUCTION

Life is a continuous journey that consists of phases such as the childhood period and the educational period in which we attend school, college or university. Then we enter the practical period, which includes finding suitable work and eventually settling down with a loved one.

We all desire to have a bright and successful future. We want to become valuable members of society, and at the same time have financial security. At this stage, we begin thinking about starting a family and owning a beautiful home so that our family can enjoy a safe and peaceful life.

In the global village in which we live today, people often migrate to other countries in search of a better future. As part of this trend, people continue to move and settle in Canada. This migration typically involves some social and financial challenges. In the beginning, people often reside in rental units. However with time, hard work and favourable circumstances, they naturally wish to take the next steps in life and consider buying their dream home. This is a very positive, constructive and healthy mindset to have.

The purchase of a home is one of the biggest and most expensive decisions in our lives. However, just as the saying goes, "no risk, no gain." We have to think positive for our future. In order to make our dreams a reality, we need to start somewhere and take that first step. A great Chinese philosopher, Lao Tzu said in *Tao Te Ching*, "A journey of a thousand miles begins with a single step." We may face many challenges and difficulties along the way, but "in the middle of difficulty lies opportunity," as Albert Einstein said. Fulfilling this vision of leaving behind the rental unit and buying our own dream home will not only be one of the most rewarding experiences of our lives, but will also be a very exciting journey, indeed!

The journey of life will always continue, but your dreams may be closer to reality than you think! For all those people who wish to explore, whether now or later, all the factors of buying (and selling) a home, I have provided an in-depth analysis. In the course of this book, I address the following core questions:

- Why should we buy a house?
- What are the benefits and responsibilities of buying a house?
- What type of house should we buy?
- Where should we purchase our dream home?
- What is a suitable method to buy our dream home?
- What is the minimum amount of money we need?

Although all of these questions are very important, in this chapter I will focus only on points related to why we should buy a house and what its benefits and responsibilities are.

ADVANTAGES OF HOMEOWNERSHIP

Homeownership has many advantages. Some of them have positive social benefits, while others have financial benefits.

• PEACE OF MIND:

Many people wish to get the best education and training possible in order to serve their countries and achieve a high social status. They also wish to live in the house they have always wanted. During the last 25 years, many people have migrated to Canada to settle. They often live in rental units and pay major portions of their hard-earned income on rent every month. People who think about the future and the long-term effects of their actions elect to buy a home if feasible. Doing this helps them attain peace of mind, knowing they are not throwing away their money on rent. Instead, they invest it for a bright future.

• FAMILY SAFETY AND SECURITY:

Long-term thinkers buy their houses as early as possible and prove to be wise people. They reside in good neighborhoods and provide safety and security for their families and children. This sense of security translates into both comfort and confidence for these families, especially the children.

• SOCIAL STATUS AND RESPECT:

The houses are mostly situated in good, residential neighborhoods and prestigious areas with esteemed schools. The parents and children feel comfortable, confident and respected living in these homes;

a better lifestyle increases their sense of respect and dignity in society. Renters and homeowners have different views and perspectives.

- ### PERSONAL FREEDOM:

Being a homeowner means you can enjoy freedom, peace of mind and the ability to live without any unnecessary restrictions. Homeowners can live the way they like and make changes in their homes in any way they please. Homeowners can also sell or rent the house according to their personal needs.

- ### ENJOYMENT AND HEALTH:

After purchasing a house, we have to work hard physically to maintain our homes. Cleaning, decorating, gardening and landscaping are some of the activities we have to undertake in order to maintain our homes. All of these activities and hobbies provide us enjoyment and good health; a healthy mind resides in a healthy body.

- ### COMPULSORY SAVING:

We learn from experience that earning money is not as difficult as spending it *wisely*. It would give us peace of mind to save some money, put it in a savings account, and then buy a home, make the regular payments and get the necessary equity.

- ### RENTING VS. OWNING:

To put things into perspective, consider this: People who live in rental units throughout their lives can purchase approximately four homes from the total rent money they will pay. This is because the property value appreciates greatly with the passage of time.

• TAX BENEFITS:

Living in Canada, we are fortunate enough to enjoy personal freedom, self-respect and dignity. Although we have to pay taxes for the country and for public welfare, the citizens of this country are taken care of according to their needs. The government encourages the public to buy real estate and facilitates the process of buying homes. Homeowners get many tax benefits and enjoy tax-free capital gain from selling their principal residence.

• VALUE APPRECIATION:

Real estate value increases everywhere and in all countries, but especially in Canada. According to Statistics Canada, during the past 25 years, approximately 250,000 people have migrated to Canada every year — and they all need a place to live. Due to the high demand for houses in Canada, real estate value is drastically increasing every year. Therefore, homeowners can both enjoy peaceful living and get financial benefits.

• BETTER CREDIT RATING:

In the case of purchasing our homes, we have to make regular payments of mortgages to the bank; financial institutions value your good creditworthiness and consider you a reliable customer based on this maintained credit. With good credit, banks can provide you further loans or a high line of credit without hesitation.

Although homeownership brings us many social and financial benefits, there are also numerous responsibilities and obligations that follow the benefits. We have to make regular payments to the lender and pay utility bills for heating, electricity, water and others. We have to continually pay our monthly home-insurance premiums for risk coverage. We have to maintain our home repairs as needed, as well as keep up with landscaping and improving home exteriors in the summer months—although gardening can be very enjoyable! Snow removal and cleaning is a necessity in the winter. Nevertheless, the responsibilities pertaining to a home are outweighed by the benefits and enjoyment one receives from owning one. I hope you gained some insight about the advantages and responsibilities of purchasing a home. Whenever you make up your mind to purchase your dream home, I hope you can make use of this valuable information during your exciting journey!

CHAPTER 2

WHICH KIND OF HOME SHOULD WE BUY?

In the first chapter, we discussed why we should buy our homes, what the benefits are, and what responsibilities come with homeownership. It is clear that, instead of living in a rented home or apartment for a long time, it is better to buy our own home as it can bring us a financial gain as well as peace of mind. The next question to ask is, *which kind of home should we buy?*

In this regard, we should keep in mind the following points:

DREAM HOME

Every person has his or her own imagination, specific needs and differing priorities. We buy our homes for peaceful and enjoyable living. Therefore, a dream home is one that fulfills our needs and desires within our capacity. It is typically a medium-sized house—not too congested and not over-sized. You should avoid buying an unnecessarily huge house that is beyond your needs and would be a burden to maintain and afford. In fact, a moderate way of living is ideal. At this stage, we should think logically, control our passions and prefer a suitable home that is feasible to afford and better to enjoy.

• LOCATION:

It is very important to remember location in the process of purchasing your home. You should buy your home in a location that makes your life easy and gives you peace of mind. Keep in mind that a good neighborhood has schools, shopping centres, access to transportation nearby and a close proximity to your workplace. Living in a good location not only gives you peace and enjoyment, but also time to appreciate the value of your property. We must consider our needs, requirements, budget and preferred location before purchasing a home.

• KINDS OF HOMES:

In every country homes are built according to local circumstances, weather, public demands and trends. Each type of property has pros and cons. Therefore, we should make this important and crucial decision with much care. The following types of homes are usually available in the market to buy and sell.

High-rise condominiums: High towers and buildings of multiple stories are very common and popular. In a condo building, each unit is owned by an individual owner, but a condo corporation authority organizes, supervises and maintains the building overall, and a maintenance fee is charged monthly to each unit owner. These condominium projects are on full boom in Toronto.

Townhouses: A building consisting of four to six units. Some are condo-townhouses. Recently developers have started building free-hold townhouses, which are very popular and in high demand. The individual owners maintain their own homes and do not pay any maintenance fees.

Semi-detached houses: A building consisting of two houses with a common wall between the two, as well as a driveway (common or private). These homes are less expensive but limit privacy. These days semis are being built more often, almost fifty percent of the time, because they are cheaper to afford. Therefore, there is a higher demand for them.

Detached houses: A house that is built with an independent structure and has full privacy. These houses are also very popular and are favourites among buyers and investors. Due to high demand, these houses are being built and sold at very high prices. They are constructed in different sizes, but between 1500 to 2500 square feet are common sizes.

• STYLES OF HOMES:

There are various styles of homes being built and sold. Every style has its own importance and value. Consumers have their own likes and dislikes, intentions, wishes and specific needs, so they need to decide on which type of house is perfect for them and their family. When the circumstances change as time passes, they can sell their current home and buy a new one.

The following styles of homes are currently available in the market.

- Bungalow: ground floor with full basement.
- Raised bungalow: main floor with approximately five to six stairs above ground level with semi-basement.
- Bungaloft: master at ground level and other bedrooms on the second storey with a full basement.
- Two-storey house: two floors and a full basement.
- Three, four or five level backsplits: levels with five to six steps.
- Three, four or five level sidesplits: each level with five to six steps and built towards a side.

ATTENTION FIRST-TIME BUYERS!

When you decide to buy your first house, make sure you discuss it with other homeowners, or consult a realtor. You should give your full attention and think carefully about the best kind of home for you; this way you can have a dream home that fulfills your needs and wants.

Among new construction, two-storey houses are the most popular and have a high demand. Young families with children, as well as large families, are the typical buyers of these homes. The second most popular style is the bungalow. Senior citizens are the typical buyers of bungalows.

The decision of buying a home is your own personal decision. You can discuss with your family and friends and consult a realtor, but the end decision rests in your hands. You have to choose the style according to your needs and preferences in order to enjoy it fully.

CHAPTER 3

WHAT IS THE BEST METHOD OF BUYING A HOME?

We have described in the previous two chapters why we should buy a house and which types of houses are available on the market. We also discussed how to choose the perfect house to buy for you and your family.

Now we will discuss some essential tips as well as the actual process of buying a home. This way your important and exciting journey can be a smooth and pleasant one, full of enjoyment. In regards to finding your dream home, you have two options available:

- **OPTION 1: EDUCATE YOURSELF**

You search and look for the perfect house. You can make use of newspapers, magazines, radio ads and websites to look for a home. In other words, you go on this journey alone. You can consult with your friends and family on your purchases. You should keep in mind that this is one of the most important and expensive decisions you will make in your life. During this exciting journey to your dream house, you have to go through different stages, take various steps, deal with many people and pass through different legal matters, issues and complications. You could face difficulties and challenges as a first-time buyer due to the lack of experience and relevant knowledge. However, we cannot deny the fact of "no risk, no gain."

- **OPTION 2: GET PROFESSIONAL HELP**

You can contact an experienced realtor for the purchase of your home and protect yourself from various complications and difficulties. If you elect to take this approach, it may be a wise decision as it will remove many complications. A realtor will give you full step by step guidance. The selection of a realtor is also a very crucial decision as it will determine whether you get the best quality of service.

SELECTING THE BEST REALTOR

For the selection of a good realtor, you should contact at least two or three real estate professionals. Have interviews one by one, collect information and ask for references from their past clients. Then analyze everything you have learned about them and choose the most competent and experienced realtor who you feel would be an honest and sincere counsellor.

The importance of a realtor is just like a doctor, a lawyer or an accountant who will be assisting you with some of the most important decisions in your life. Decide very carefully in selecting the right realtor. Then you need to have trust and full confidence in your chosen realtor and depend on him or her. Make a verbal or written agreement and act upon it sincerely. As a result, your realtor will give you full attention, show complete responsibility and provide you their best professional services sincerely, honestly and confidently. This way your journey to your dream home will be exciting, pleasant and worry-free.

VARIOUS STEPS DURING THE SEARCH FOR YOUR DREAM HOME

• MEETING WITH A REALTOR:

When you have decided to go along with a realtor for the search of your dream house, you need to set up a detailed meeting with the realtor. This meeting can take place at the office of the realtor or your own residence. This meeting is a very important stepping-stone for the fulfilment of your objective of finding your dream home. Accordingly, it should be held in a peaceful and pleasant atmosphere. You must have full confidence, trust and satisfaction with your realtor. You should provide the realtor with all the details and circumstances of your potential purchase. Tell them about your family needs, requirements, desires and financial sources; provide facts and figures. Then your realtor will be in a perfect position to give you the best advice and suggestions. Make sure to include your family members in this meeting and decide together which kind of house is perfect for you. Also, remember to discuss the minimum and maximum amount that you are willing to spend.

- ## HOME SEARCH:

When you have decided what type of house you want to buy and the location you like, searching for it will become much easier for your realtor. Alternatively, you can also search for the home on your own. If you happen to find a suitable home in a nice location, tell your realtor to book an appointment for a viewing. Your realtor spends a lot of time and effort to search for your dream home and set up appointments for you to view the homes, so you must give the appointments importance. You must be punctual and arrive on time. Try not to cancel appointments unless you have unavoidable circumstances and genuine reasons.

- ## PREPARATIONS AND PRESENTATIONS:

If and when you find a house that is suitable in all aspects, then instead of overthinking and waiting, prepare your offer. If you are looking for homes and dealing with all of this on your own, it is better to involve a lawyer. If you are working with a realtor, he or she will prepare your offer and pre-set the necessary and most appropriate conditions accordingly. Then the realtor will present this offer of purchase to the home seller through a listing broker, and will negotiate the price along with the terms and conditions, and finalize the agreement of purchase and sale.

• SUBMISSION OF DEPOSIT:

When sellers and buyers agree upon a certain price, the deal will become final. The agreed deposit amount is manually submitted within 24 hours to the listing broker's office in the form of a bank deposit or certified cheque. In the case of a private sale, the deposit can be submitted to the seller or their lawyer's trust account.

• MORTGAGE APPROVAL:

In the process of purchasing your home, mortgage approval and financing are among the most important steps. You should talk to experienced professionals in this field to get the best advice. You may contact your bank, realtor, real estate lawyer or any mortgage broker to get full information and guidance to make an informed decision. Usually, buyers consider utilizing the services of a mortgage broker because brokers have access to many different lenders in the mortgage field. They shop around and negotiate the best rates on your behalf. Sometimes mortgage brokers charge a fee, but mostly they receive their commission from the lenders.

• HOME INSPECTION:

After you get approved for a mortgage, you need a qualified home inspector. You can select any good inspector who is available in the market, or you can ask your realtor to get the inspector with the best price and quality. Qualified home inspectors usually spend two to three hours to complete this job in your presence. They provide guidance and information, and prepare a full report of the home inspection for your record. They charge their fee according to the property, but usually the rates are between $300–500 plus HST (Harmonized Sales Tax).

- ## WAIVING THE CONDITIONS:

In the process of purchasing your home, there are usually two conditions included in the "Agreement of Purchase and Sale." These two conditions are finance approval and home inspection. This means that an approval of mortgage and a satisfactory home inspection report are necessary. Both conditions are waived at a set date, and the deal will be consolidated then.

- ## ATTAINING A LAWYER'S SERVICE:

When the "Agreement of Purchase and Sale" is completed and the deal is finalized by waiving all the conditions, a copy of the agreement is provided to an appointed lawyer. The lawyer will act on behalf of the buyer in this transaction. He or she will contact the buyer to set the meeting. The lawyer has to discharge all responsibilities and financial matters relating to the transaction. The lawyer will collect the down payment and closing costs from the buyer and deposit it in a trust account.

- ## POSSESSION OF THE HOUSE:

Your lawyer has to fulfill all necessary requirements and take the necessary steps to get in contact with the seller's lawyer. On the closing date, your lawyer will pay the balance owed to the seller's lawyer, collect the keys of the house and hand them over to you.

This important and exciting journey will come to an end, and you will have achieved your goal: buying your dream home! On this happy occasion, I congratulate you from the bottom of my heart. I pray to God that He may bless this home for you and your family, and give you happiness in your future life!

TIPS TO REMEMBER WHEN BUYING A HOUSE

+ Attend a first-time home buyer's seminar.
+ Know how much you can afford.
+ Prioritize your needs and wants.
+ Explore mortgage options and the quantity of your mortgage loan.
+ Get knowledge of first-time home buyer's programs.
+ Find and select the right realtor.
+ Understand the offer process.
+ Get the right home inspector service.
+ Read and understand what you are signing.
+ Think positive and look forward.
+ Be a fair thinker.
+ Buy an affordable and practical house.

CHAPTER 4

HOW CAN WE MAINTAIN OUR HOME?

In the past three chapters, we have gone through some questions in detail: Why should we buy a house? Out of the available houses on the market, which type of house should we buy? How should we purchase our homes?

Now we will discuss an important topic: maintaining and looking after your dream home so that it can be enjoyed fully. Regular inspections and maintenance are important in ensuring that your property is in excellent condition. Early detection of defects will prevent permanent damage to your property and lower potential repair costs. In this regard, I recommend that you pay attention and implement the following important points:.

- **ATTENTION TO HOME INSPECTION:**

Most of the time we inspect the home that we are going to buy. We hire a qualified home inspector who spends several hours and prepares a report for our satisfaction and guidance. In the past, it has been observed that homebuyers consider the home inspection a formality and an unnecessary thing, so they do not give it their full attention and sometimes do not care to be present when the inspection is taking place. They simply tell their realtor to take care of this important responsibility. This is an extremely important step during the purchase of your dream home, and I suggest people be present at the inspection along with their family members. Take full advantage of the guidance and important tips provided by the qualified home inspector.

- **TRANSFER OF UTILITIES:**

After the closing of your home, ensure that accounts of electricity, water and gas have been transferred over to your name. This is usually done by the lawyer, but sometimes buyers have to contact utility companies themselves.

- **ATTENTION TO FURNACE:**

This is an important element of a house as it serves to provide a warm place in the winter and a cool place in the summer. For this reason, it is very important to maintain the furnace to get optimal performance and save on consumption. For better results, it is good to check the air filter regularly and replace it when needed. There are two types of filters available at the moment. One is disposable, inexpensive and needs to be changed every two to three months. The second is an expensive filter, but it lasts a lifetime and needs to be cleaned every two to three months.

- **ATTENTION TO AIR CONDITIONING UNIT:**

Ensure the air conditioning unit is properly sized for your home. Having a unit that is either too big or too small for a home can be highly inefficient. A split unit could be more energy efficient. You must clean the air filters regularly and have the air conditioner inspected annually. The annual inspection may extend the life of the equipment and help to save money by reducing your energy bills.

- **MAINTAIN DOORS AND WINDOWS:**

We should keep an eye on the doors and windows of our homes. Make sure they are all in good condition. If you observe any cracks, seal them with some tiling material to avoid the wastage of energy. All of the windows and doors should be cleaned and lubricated every year for optimal performance.

- **SAVE ON ENERGY BILLS:**

You should avoid unnecessary usage of electricity, water and gas. By using energy carefully, not only do you save our natural resources, but you save and control your utilities and costs as well. Ensure your family members know about the saving of energy. Similarly, you should read the instructions and act upon the guidance you receive from the local city authority to save energy costs by observing times and rates.

- ## CLEANING AND HOUSEKEEPING:

Cleanliness is a crucial part of your physical and spiritual life. If you keep your home clean with the intention of maintaining your physical and spiritual well-being, you will become the recipient of many blessings. You will also enjoy the peace of mind of having a clean atmosphere to live in. To keep your home clean, you should use a vacuum cleaner regularly, perhaps every day if you have carpeting in your house. It is advisable to have a thorough cleaning done once a week, whether you do it on your own or have your home professionally cleaned. Also, make use of a central vacuum if it is available.

- ## DISCARD UNNECESSARY ITEMS:

People make many purchases in their daily lives, but as time passes, some of these purchases become old, out of fashion or break. The items that are not in good condition should be properly disposed of. The remaining good items not in use can be sold or dropped off at the nearest donation cart for the benefit of the less fortunate.

- ## UTILIZE THE BASEMENT:

The underground level of a house is called the basement. Usually, brand new homes come with an unfinished basement; some older homes have a finished basement. You can make great use of this part of your home. If you want to use it for financial gain, you can finish it and make it a living space. This way it can become a rental suite after having fulfilled the local city requirements. On the other hand, you can finish it as a recreation room for your family get-togethers, and for the children to play. The whole family can enjoy it and have a good time.

If you give due attention and act upon the various important points mentioned above, you will be able to reap the benefits of owning your dream home.

CHAPTER 5

WHAT IS A MORTGAGE & HOW CAN WE PAY IT OFF FASTER?

Now let's discuss an important topic: home mortgage. In fact, it is near impossible for us to purchase a home with full cash payment. So we pay some amount of the price as a down payment and the rest of the balance is borrowed from the bank to pay the seller of the house. Then we pay back the bank in regular installments.

WHAT IS A MORTGAGE?

Generally, a mortgage is a claim upon the real property given by the borrower (owner) of the property to the bank as a security for all the money borrowed, and it is registered in the land registry office. In return, the owner makes the required regular payments to the lender. The owner has the right to discharge the mortgage from the title once the full debt is paid off. In regards to mortgage, the following terms are very important:

- ### AMORTIZATION:

If we borrow money from a financial institution, we have to repay it within a specific time; this is called the amortization period. It could last 25-30 years, more or less, depending on how much you pay and how often. The shorter the amortization period, the less interest you have to pay, and you pay your debt off faster. On the other hand, it is easier to afford a longer amortization period even though the total interest is higher, because you do not pay as much per installment.

- ### RATE OF INTEREST:

This is a percentage of interest that a lender charges on the amount of money borrowed. Usually the banks provide mortgage at fixed rates, but sometimes the lenders offer variable rates that fluctuate with the prime rate. Nowadays there is a lot of competition in the mortgage business sector, so we can negotiate for the best possible interest rates and the most attractive terms and conditions.

- ### TERM:

This is the time period that our mortgage is guaranteed for by the lender. The lender cannot ask for full repayment unless the borrower is in default of the periodic payments.

- ### OPEN MORTGAGE:

In an open mortgage, we are allowed to make extra payments in addition to our regular payments without any penalty. However, the banks charge a higher interest rate in an open mortgage term.

- ### CLOSED MORTGAGE:

Usually we pay a low interest rate in a closed mortgage, but we do not have flexibility in making changes in the term. If we do, the bank will charge us a penalty.

- ### PRE-PAYMENTS:

Advance payments made to the bank under the mortgage contract can be full or partial, of all or part of the principle. It should be separate from the regular payments. Usually, lenders offer a 20 percent prepayment option without charging a penalty and this is paid fully against the principle amount.

- ### PAYMENT OPTIONS:

Today financial institutions offer different payment options to the borrowers. We can make the payments weekly, bi-weekly or monthly. In addition, we can increase our regular payments.

• ASSUMPTION:

We can assume the existing mortgage provided for the homeowner if the lender allowed for it. By assuming mortgage, we can save some expenses of appraisal fees, legal fees and survey costs. It is beneficial for a buyer if the existing mortgage has a lower interest rate than the current rate. In addition, it is good for sellers because they may save some penalty charges if it is discharged before the maturity period.

PRIVILEGES OF MORTGAGE

In Canada, there is a tough competition in the mortgage business; all financial institutions offer mortgages to consumers at very attractive terms and conditions to gain more business and a better reputation in the market. There are some rights for consumers mentioned in the mortgage agreement. Similarly, there are some privileges offered by the lenders to the borrowers. To take advantage of these privileges, we have to be very smart and strategic in dealing with lenders. We have another option in this regard: if we get the services of a sincere and reliable mortgage broker, it could be beneficial.

Here are some privileges usually offered to us by lenders:

• PREPAYMENT:

Some banks allow us to prepay a portion of our mortgage before the term is matured. Usually the lenders allow us to pay back up to 20 percent of the original mortgage amount every year. They do not charge any penalty on this prepayment. This extra payback amount is fully deducted from the loan balance without any interest charges.

• RENEWAL:

Some borrowers think their mortgage contract will be renewed automatically after the maturity of their term. This is not the case. The banks or lenders usually renew the mortgage temporarily for a short period, if we have not decided the expiration date of our mortgage terms.

• TRANSFER OF PRIVILEGES:

Lenders often provide a transfer of privilege to the seller if the seller would like to pass this on to the potential buyer. However, the lenders still hold the original borrower liable if the mortgage is in default by the one who assumed it. Therefore, we must check and verify the credibility of our potential buyers. This privilege is very beneficial for buyers because they can save various expenses, especially if the rates of interest are low.

• PORTABLE PRIVILEGE:

If we sell our present home, we have to pay off the mortgage balance as well as some penalty, and then we can obtain a new mortgage for the next house. However, if the current mortgage documents have the provision of portability, we can transfer our mortgage towards our new purchase and save a lot of expenses and other processing formalities. Ensure you have the provision of portability in your current mortgage document, especially a low interest rate. It is crucial to obtain the benefit of this privilege.

HOW TO GET A MORTGAGE

We need a loan to purchase our homes, and so we have two options:

• OPTION 1: CONTACT A BANK

You can contact the bank yourself and negotiate a mortgage for the purchase of your home. Experience shows that usually it is not as beneficial to directly negotiate and acquire a mortgage from a financial institution yourself. The bank employees work for their employer's benefits, and so the borrowers rarely enjoy attractive terms and conditions of their mortgage. The biggest difficulty most people have in shopping for their own mortgage is that they do not know how to ask the right questions or choose the best terms to fit their needs.

- ## OPTION 2: CONTACT A MORTGAGE BROKER

You can rely on mortgage brokers and get their professional services, mostly free of charge. Mortgage brokers have more experience and professional knowledge than an ordinary consumer does, and so they can obtain a mortgage with the best terms and conditions. Mortgage brokers have access to many lenders and loan programs. Usually they submit your loan applications to many lenders and shop around for the most competitive mortgage rates and attractive conditions. Then you can decide which option to use.

ADVANTAGES OF PAYING OFF YOUR MORTGAGE FASTER

- You will have peace of mind when the mortgage is all paid off.
- Decrease in daily expenses: your life will be easier and more comfortable if the huge responsibility of mortgage is off your shoulders.
- Fearless unemployment: you will be worry-free when the mortgage is paid off.
- Strong determination: saving and paying off the mortgage will give you strong determination.
- Strong relationship in married couples: early and faster mortgage payment will bring happiness to married couples to enjoy life.
- Financial freedom and worry-free life: we can enjoy life if our expenses are less than our income.
- Tax benefits: we can enjoy tax benefits.

+ Contract on unnecessary expenses: if we have focus on paying off our mortgage faster, we can avoid unnecessary expenses and lavish spending.

+ Comfortable in financial matters: our lives will be a lot easier and comfortable if financially we are well off.

SMART STEPS TO PAY OFF YOUR MORTGAGE

Most people like to fulfill their obligations and responsibilities so they feel comfortable and free from any kind of burden. The purchase of a home is a basic need, which can be achieved easily in Canada. However, we have to take care of financial obligations after the purchase. Here are some smart steps we can take to pay the house mortgage faster and fulfil this financial obligation.

• FULL AWARENESS:

Whenever we take a step, we should pray and seek help and guidance from our God. Then we should get full information and consider the positive and negative effects. We must understand our obligations. In other words, we should make an informed decision and then put our trust in God.

• MORTGAGE DETAILS:

It is almost impossible to buy a home without having a mortgage to pay, and so it is very important to become educated and attain maximum knowledge about mortgages. Apart from the banks, you can contact your family, friends, realtors, real estate lawyers and mortgage brokers to get advice and information.

- ## GETTING A MORTGAGE WITH ATTRACTIVE TERMS:

We can contact banks as well as mortgage brokers to get a mortgage for our home. Compare the terms and conditions and interest rates from all sources. Then take the mortgage with the best rates and most attractive conditions.

- ## PAYMENT FREQUENCY:

We can make regular payments of our mortgage on a weekly, bi-weekly or monthly basis. It is better to consult with an experienced mortgage broker. I have learned from my experiences that the bi-weekly option of payment has been the most beneficial. The extra bi-weekly payments are counted 100 percent for the principle amount payment, which can result in paying off the home many years sooner.

- ## EXTRA PREPAYMENTS:

If you can save some money and pay extra in addition to your regular payments, it will reduce your principle amount every year. If your financial circumstances permit, you can double up your regular payments. I have seen some homebuyers who have paid off their mortgage fully in less than five years, became debt-free and are enjoying their lives peacefully.

- ## VARIABLE RATES:

At the time of obtaining a mortgage, we should try our best to go for variable rates. Lenders mostly suggest fixed rates, but in the long term, variable rates can be more beneficial. You can compare both options and then decide.

- ## USE OF EXTRA INCOME:

Whenever you receive some extra income (e.g., tax refund), try to pay it towards your mortgage account.

- ## BASEMENT APARTMENT:

If you have extra space in your basement that you are not using, you can convert it into a living space and make it a rental unit. Extra income from that unit can be used to pay off your mortgage.

- ## MAKE A LUMP-SUM PAYMENT:

If it is difficult to make extra payments on a regular basis, you can make a lump-sum payment every year.

All of these steps mentioned are valuable suggestions. If you can act upon some of them, you will be able to pay off your mortgage faster, become debt-free earlier and enjoy life.

CHAPTER 6

HOW CAN WE BEAUTIFY OUR HOMES?

In this chapter, we will discuss how we can beautify and decorate our dream homes and what positive effects beautification yields. We can divide this topic into two parts.

INTERNAL BEAUTIFICATION

By the grace of God, when we are blessed with our homes, we wish to make it a beautiful home and yearn to enjoy it fully. If you give some attention and act upon the following points, not only will you be able to enjoy your home, but your guests and relatives will also appreciate your efforts and good work.

- ## CLEANLINESS:

Home cleanliness and maintaining a tidy condition is very important because it shows a quality living standard. You will feel better about yourself and will achieve physical and spiritual pleasure.

- ## SELECTION OF PAINTS AND SHADES:

Every person has likes and dislikes when it comes to shades of paint. Some people like dark shades on their walls, and others like lighter colours. Children usually decorate their rooms with shades of their choices. Most homeowners prefer white or light shade paint in their homes. In fact, the moderate way is the best lifestyle of living. Very dark shades look congested and narrow, and white looks too simple and ordinary. The selection of high-quality paint with a light or medium colour will increase beauty and make your home look spacious.

- ## DOORS, WINDOWS AND CABINETS:

If we give due attention to internal doors, windows and kitchen cabinets, it will add value and attraction to the dream home. By using high-quality products, we can decorate the house with a new look and it will be a nice change. The visual volume of the house will also increase.

- ## CURTAINS AND BLINDS:

In the decoration of our homes, window curtains and blinds are very important. The selection of an appropriate colour scheme of curtains beautifies our home and makes it more appealing. Shopping has become very easy and convenient. You can even shop online and get products delivered to your door in a few days.

• FLOORS:

People have their own likes and dislikes, as mentioned before. Some people like carpeted floors, others like hardwood and some prefer laminate floors. Flooring in a house is the most used area, so we have to select it very carefully, keeping in mind its practical usage. We can consult with an experienced floor installer or a designer.

• SELECTING FURNITURE:

Furniture plays an important role in the beautification of our homes. Suitable colour, design and size of our furniture will definitely add beauty to our homes. In addition, furniture can be matched with floors and curtains or blinds to add further appeal

• COOKING AT HOME:

Most of us cook food in our homes. Although there is a lot of labour and hardship involved in the preparation of food at home, we can save a lot financially. Heavy cooking may cause an odour or smell, which is not a healthy atmosphere in our homes. There are many precautionary steps we can take to overcome this. For example, you could install a high-quality range hood over the stove in the kitchen. Similarly, during the cooking process, you can have cross ventilation and fresh air by keeping the doors and windows open for a short time.

POSITIVE EFFECTS OF INTERNAL DECORATION AND CLEANLINESS

+ We can attain physical and spiritual pleasure because cleanliness is an essential part of human life.
+ A clean atmosphere and decorated home will bring mental satisfaction and happiness.
+ Any good action and movement has blessings. Physical work and hardship to maintain your home will make you active and healthy, both mentally and physically.
+ When friends and relatives visit your home, your efforts of decorating will be appreciated, and your guests will be impressed.
+ A well-decorated and maintained home will have more value and price.
+ A good living standard and modern lifestyle will elevate your respect and dignity.
+ An organized lifestyle will create good working habits and confidence in your children, resulting in a better upbringing for them. They will develop excellent habits and skills to succeed in life.
+ The concept of decoration and beautification will create a lot of business in the country. More production sectors will be developed, and more jobs will be created as well.

EXTERNAL BEAUTIFICATION AND MAINTENANCE

The external portion of the house includes the front entrance, porch, garage door, driveway, external walls, windows, roof, and the front, side and back yards. There is a tremendous amount of physical work and hardship involved to beautify and maintain the external part of the house. But collectively, family members can easily handle this assignment.

The home is an important and expensive asset of our lives so we will have peace of mind and happiness if we live in a well-maintained and beautifully decorated house. Here are some ideas for external beautification.

- ### FRONT ENTRANCE AND PORCH:

With the passage of time, colours usually fade or stain with continuous use. If the front door is old or stained, you can replace it with a new door, or you can give it a new look with fresh paint. Similarly, paint the porch with a high-quality exterior paint. As a result, your house will look more attractive and will give a good first impression.

- ### GARAGE DOOR AND DRIVEWAY:

The garage door and driveway in front of your home are very important elements for first impressions. Give your home a new look and good first impression by repainting the garage door and driveway every year or every few years.

- ### FRONT YARD:

We have to manage long winters and seemingly short summers in Canada. We have a very brief season for landscaping and growing flowers. We must take advantage of the few summer months we have and enjoy the hobby of gardening, which is a healthy usage of our time and also adds beauty to the home.

- ### EXTERNAL WALLS:

The external walls of the home are very important for protection and security from severe weather and other conditions. Usually the external walls are made of bricks, stucco or vinyl, which wear down as time goes on and require some repairs and touch-ups. Many homeowners are active in the beginning of summer, but we must give due attention and check the exterior walls all year round. We need to repair any cracks or other physical imperfections in the external parts of the home. In addition, we can make use of different shades of paint to make the external walls look more attractive.

• EXTERNAL DOORS AND WINDOWS:

We should clean the doors and windows every year in the summer; wash them with water and a suitable cleaner. Also, paint the external part of the doors and windows, which will make the home more attractive and extend its life.

• BACKYARD:

The backyard is a portion of the lot, an open space that is kept behind the main building, or on the right or left side of the house. This open space depends on the style of the house. Usually corner houses and detached houses have bigger lots, whereas townhouses and semi-detached homes consist of smaller lots. We can make use of this open space of our homes according to our wishes, needs or hobbies. We can use part of this open space for concrete or interlocked floors, a wooden deck or for landscaping and gardening. We can even install a swimming pool.

As the homeowner, you are free to utilize your backyard space however you prefer. However, ensure your yard looks beautiful, neat, clean and well-organized.

POSITIVE EFFECTS OF EXTERNAL DECORATION

+ It will create a good first impression if your home is maintained properly.
+ The age and value of your house will increase.
+ A house is our nest and is a valuable asset. If it is taken care of properly, the owners will have peace of mind and happiness.

✦   Matters of maintenance and beautification of our homes require a lot of physical effort. It will bring positive effects to our physical and mental health.

✦   Maintaining and decorating the home will be good for the creative part of our minds.

CHAPTER 7

HOW CAN WE ENJOY GARDENING?

I am pleased to present some information about the interesting and very useful hobby of gardening and farming.

BENEFITS OF HOBBIES

+ Peace of mind: hobbies take away worries of life.
+ Reveals a passion/talent: you might discover you have a talent you were unaware of just from pursuing a hobby.

+ Networking tool: it's an excellent conversation starter that can reflect your personality and reduce anxiety.
+ Relaxation: hobbies often provide a perfect way to relax your mind when you come home after working.
+ Enhance employment opportunities.
+ It is a source of learning new skills.
+ There are positive effects on your physical and mental health.
+ It brings happiness and satisfactions to individuals.

OUR HOMES AND GARDENING

After we purchase our home and start living in it peacefully, we need to be employed continuously or have a steady income in order to fulfil our responsibilities and our daily cost of living. We have a very busy life in Canada. The financial system here provides us with opportunities to grow, establish ourselves and achieve whatever we wish in our lives: an amazing home, beautiful furniture, a perfect car. However, later on, we have to make payments to the lenders for all of these luxuries and needs. Most of our time is spent at our jobs so that we earn money and pay bills, but even then, we can spare some time for ourselves. Now it is up to us to utilize the time we have for ourselves effectively, whether we spend it maintaining our home or spending it with our families.

In the previous chapter, I mentioned that free-hold properties consist of a constructed area and a vacant area around the house. You can make use of this vacant land according to your likes or interests. Although Canada has a long winter and a short summer, we can still take advantage of this brief summer every year if we have interesting and useful hobbies.

We can enjoy our favourite hobby in our spare time according to our wishes, needs or interests. Out of these hobbies, gardening and farming in our backyard are interesting and mentally satisfying. This hobby can be divided into two parts.

GARDENING: GROWING VEGETABLES AND FRUITS

This hobby is typically enjoyed in the backyard of our home. We can reserve some portion of the backyard to grow vegetable and fruits. You have to dig this area with a shovel and make it soft, take away all of the grass roots and mix in some fertilizer. It will be made better if we do this at the end of summer or just before winter starts. As soon as the winter season is over, you should dig and make a soft bed. Then you can buy and plant the fruits and/or vegetables seeds. Ensure you continuously water plants as needed. When the plants are grown, clean and uproot the grass roots, once again, so that the vegetables and fruits grow faster. Within a few weeks, your labour will bear fruit, and you can enjoy fresh vegetables and fruits every day.

ADVANTAGES OF GARDENING

+ You will have peace of mind.
+ You will enjoy a nice sleep at night as a result of your healthy physical exertion.
+ The physical activity helps you maintain an active lifestyle, and therefore improves your overall health.
+ This interesting hobby creates a sense of achievement.
+ It creates a close relationship between human and nature.
+ You can learn a new skill and art.
+ It saves you money, enables you to use your time wisely and provides you with fresh food.
+ It will beautify your garden and environment.
+ It provides food for the birds and animals as well.
+ Landscaping will enhance the beauty of your home and increase its value by up to 20 percent.

+ It reveals your creativity.
+ It strengthens the relationship of love and affection within individual families.
+ Gardening adds beauty to the environment and makes the neighbourhood attractive.

LANDSCAPING

Landscaping is a very interesting and healthy activity. We can beautify our backyards and lots by growing flowers, vegetables and various colourful bushes. Gardening is usually considered an activity of peace and satisfaction.

• AIMS AND OBJECTIVES OF BACKYARD LANDSCAPING:

There are different aims and objectives of beautifying our backyards.

+ Play area for children
+ Outdoor accommodation for pets
+ Area for parties and entertainment
+ Peaceful seclusion
+ Healthy activities (e.g. swimming)
+ Growing plants, flowers and trees

TIPS AND SUGGESTIONS FOR SUCCESSFUL GARDENING

+ Preplanning is very important for success.
+ Use good quality soil and fertilizer in the bed.
+ Make groups and grow different plants accordingly.
+ Select plants that need less care.
+ Raise the bed to grow vegetables and plants, or use containers.

+ Use a sprinkler for irrigation as it saves water.
+ A garden shed can be very helpful in the backyard.
+ Buy appropriate gardening tools; protect and store them in the shed.
+ Use gardening wheels (trolley) for convenience.
+ Create interest and encourage your children to help you in gardening.

CHAPTER 8

HOW CAN SOLAR ENERGY BE USEFUL IN OUR HOMES?

If we think about the topic of solar energy in our homes, many questions arise in our minds. For example, what is solar energy? What is its importance in our daily lives? What are the benefits and uses of solar energy? How is solar energy important and beneficial to homeowners? What is the amount of investment required for the installation of solar energy? What is the procedure to get it installed?

- ## SOLAR ENERGY AND POWER:

Solar is a word derived from Latin, which means sun. The sun is a major source of heat, and it is impossible to survive without it. The sun generates both energy and light. Besides solar energy, there are other secondary sources, such as wind power and wave energy, that are used for continuous power generation on earth. It is estimated that the space above earth gets approximately 174 petawatts of energy from the sun's rays. Out of this energy, 30 percent goes back to outer space; the rest gets absorbed in clouds, seas and the earth. When the earth receives these rays from the sun, it increases the temperature and remains an average temperature of about 14°C.

- ## USES OF SOLAR ENERGY:

Humans are capturing solar power and making use of it in different ways: through space heating and cooling, the production of portable water by distillation, disinfection, lighting, hot water, cooking and the production of usable electricity.

- ## FUTURE OF SOLAR ENERGY:

Although the use of solar energy is still limited, scientists and researchers are spending their time and efforts on the development of this alternative power technology. Similarly, some governments of the world provide a lot of funding for the development of this useful technology, and they even offer some incentives for making advancements in the use of solar energy. Many other countries also offer incentives, providing financial assistance and full guidance to their citizens to install solar power technologies in their homes.

- ### GENERAL ADVANTAGES OF SOLAR POWER:

Solar energy is an important source of power, and many countries are focusing their efforts to implement solar energy systems in everyday life. As a result, solar energy has become an important and useful energy source, and advancements are constantly being made. Here are some advantages.

- Solar power is a natural and renewable energy source.
- It causes no pollution.
- It is noiseless and calm.
- Solar power and light are blessings from God; they are free and everlasting.
- Running a solar water pump does not require any connection of a gas or grid station.
- Users of solar energy systems will not be affected by shortages or any problems in the supply of electricity.

- ### USES OF SOLAR ENERGY IN DAILY LIFE:

Human beings are gaining many benefits from this system in their daily lives: heating of water, drying clothes, heating water in swimming pools, getting power for small machines and supplying energy to cars and airplanes.

- ### FINANCIAL BENEFITS FOR HOME OWNERS:

If we make a one-time investment to install solar power systems in our homes, we will be self-sufficient for our own use of power, and we can sell this power to local utility companies to earn long-term profit. The average cost of utility bills in an average home is approximately $6,000 annually, which can be minimized significantly by implementing solar energy systems in our homes. In addition, we can make profit by selling power to utility companies.

- ## SOLAR POWER SYSTEM AND PEACE OF MIND:

If we have installed solar systems in our homes, we do not need the services of local utility companies, and we will not be affected if there is a shortage of electricity in the area. Instead, we will be able to continue our use of solar power. Knowing we will not be affected by outages gives us peace of mind.

- ## INVESTING IN A SOLAR POWER SYSTEM:

The question arises in our minds as to how much investment is required to install a solar power system in our homes. According to experts, approximately $20,000 is needed to install a system in an average home of three to four bedrooms. It can be recovered in a few years through savings of utility bills and earnings from the sale of extra power to local power companies.

FUNDING A SOLAR POWER SYSTEM

We know solar energy is important and has many benefits. From the installation of solar power systems in our homes, we can get financial benefits and make our lives more convenient and worry-free. However, we need some money for this important investment. We can make use of the following.

- Personal sources: Upon purchasing a home, some people spend a large amount to furnish their homes because it is considered a need to do so. We should look at the installation of a solar energy system as a need as well. It can be a profitable business, so we should try to arrange funds from our personal savings or other sources.

+ Mortgage companies: You can request the same lender, who provided your home mortgage, for funds to create a solar energy system in your home. It adds value to the home; they may grant you a loan and include it in your existing mortgage balance.

+ Bank sources: Most banks offer funds to purchase a solar power system, under Ontario's "Feed-in-Tariff Program," because they expect a guaranteed income from a solar power system in 15-20 years.

INSTALLATION OF A SOLAR ENERGY SYSTEM

Keeping in mind the importance, benefits, convenience and the various uses of a solar energy system, if you think the installation of this system in your home is a worthwhile investment, you should contact a sincere and knowledgeable consultant regarding the installation of this system. This expert will give you his or her professional advice and full guidance to install the system in your home.

If you have enough technical knowledge and skill regarding solar energy systems, you can also contact your provincial power authority and local city building department to get approval of a "Feed-in-Tariff" contract and a building permit. Then you may get the services of any reputable installation company for the installation of a solar energy system in your home.

I hope you have gained some information and knowledge regarding solar energy. If you need further information and want to inquire about the installation procedure, find a sincere and experienced consultant so that you may get this valuable system installed in your homes in order to enjoy savings, convenience and comfort.

CHAPTER 9

HOW SHOULD WE SELL OUR HOME?

This chapter is about selling our homes for the best price, which is an extremely important topic. If for any reason it is time to sell our home, many questions arise: Why should we sell our home? What is an alternative? When is the best time to sell? How do we sell, and what are the steps we have to go through? What is the most effective plan to sell the house to get the highest value?

REASONS TO SELL A HOME

We buy a home according to our wishes, interests and needs, and we enjoy living in it and seeing our dreams come true. However, sometimes special circumstances force us to sell our dream home. Let us look at some of those compelling reasons or circumstances:

- **EMPLOYMENT INSTABILITY:**

Losing a job, or moving from one place to another for better economic prospect, sometimes affects our financial ability to retain the home, so we have to sell it.

- **FAMILY CIRCUMSTANCES:**

Changing family needs and circumstances are an important factor. If we have an increase in our family size, we need a larger home. If the family size has reduced due to children living separately after marriage or getting jobs, we may also want a different house. When our children reach high school or university, we sometimes need to move to a location closer to that educational institution. Or we may need to move to a place that is closer to our new job site. In some cases a family break-up or reunion, or health circumstances, require us to change our residence; sometimes people inherit a house, and as they already have a house, they proceed to sell it.

- **FINANCIAL REASONS:**

We may want to sell our house for profit when real estate prices are on the rise. A change in mortgage rates is also a factor that may provoke us to sell our house and buy a new one, on newer, more flexible and more attractive rates.

- ### CHANGE IN LIFESTYLE:

It is human nature that after the passage of time, we want a change in our living style, and this changed lifestyle may require a new or upgraded home. In some circumstances, due to our growing age, medical conditions or cultural and social developments, our lifestyles are changed and the existing houses no longer suit our new lifestyles. Sometimes we are fed up with the maintenance of our existing house, like snow removal, lawn mowing, roof leakage and other property maintenance problems. Keeping in mind the size of our family, we think a condo or apartment will be more convenient for us, so we want to sell our family home and buy a condo or apartment.

Sometimes we want to get away from urban life and wish to experience a peaceful and quiet countryside living. In some cases, people wish to have a brand new home and dispose of their existing home for a change of taste. Some people have special needs, and some desire to have a custom-made home according to their new dreams. For all or some of these reasons, people aspire to sell their existing home and buy a new one that better fits their needs and desires.

WHEN SHOULD WE SELL OUR HOME?

The answer to this question depends on the previously mentioned factors that lead us to selling our home. . The timing of selling the house also depends upon the urgency of the reasons. Sometimes the reasons are not so compelling, and the owner has time to plan and wait for the right time to sell the property. In that case, they can wait for a buyer who can offer the desired price.

According to real estate experts, there is no fixed time to buy a house, but the earlier the better. On the other hand, it is very important to study, observe and research the current market conditions, events and circumstances before selling a property.

If you are thinking of downsizing, take your time to observe the market; plan slowly and carefully. However, if you are thinking of upsizing and moving to a larger house, it is better to decide quickly instead of taking a long time to move.

If you expect an increase in mortgage interest rates, there are more chances of a market slowdown, and in such a situation, a fast and early decision of selling is more appropriate. On the other hand, a decrease in interest rates will turn the market hot and active. In that case, take your time, watch and wait for the best price.

THE BEST TIME TO SELL A HOME

Based on my experience, the best time to sell a house is in the spring. Due to a long winter in North America, especially in Canada, people have to confine themselves to their homes and rely on indoor activities. As soon as spring starts, it gives them energy, hope and desire to think about their new interests, dreams and passions to make healthy changes in their lives. Taxes are filed by the end of April, and people have the next year's fiscal targets in mind. Parents are mindful of the new school year for their children. Selling and buying a house usually takes about five to six months, and so April and May are the ideal months for selling, buying and moving to a new home.

MARKET FACTORS OF BUYING AND SELLING REAL ESTATE

Whenever you think of buying or selling real estate, first you should focus on studying the market conditions and the circumstances that affect the market conditions. The following are some important factors that must be considered before dealing with real estate.

- Buyer's Market. This is a supply and demand situation. There are fewer buyers in the market and more properties available for sale. In such a circumstance, a longer time is taken for the sale of the property, and the prices are either stagnant or downward trending. Buyers will hold on and think more, because they have a longer time to decide.

- <u>Seller's Market</u>. In this case, there are more buyers but fewer properties for sale—that is, there is more demand and less supply. In this case, the sale prices will show an upward trend in the market, and properties are sold faster. In this situation sellers are more aggressive.

- <u>Balanced Market</u>. In this situation, demand and supply are equal, and enough houses are available in the market for sale to a reasonable number of buyers. As a result, the real estate market trend is moderate. Buyers will offer a reasonable price to the sellers, and property will be sold in a reasonable time frame. There will be less aggressiveness due to lack of competition between buyers and sellers.

SHOULD WE BUY OR SELL FIRST?

This is a very complicated and sensitive decision. In fact, both sides have positive and negative effects. Usually, realtors recommend homeowners to sell first, try to set a long closing date to get enough time to look for a new home to buy, and then match the closing dates for both transactions. This is the best, most appropriate and least complicated option of selling and buying a home. Sometimes your house is sold but you cannot find an appropriate new home. In this situation, you can use the option of temporary rental units.

If the real estate market is hot and shows an upward trend, look for a house to buy first and set a long closing date. In this case, you can put your current house in the market for sale. It will be less stressful, less complicated and less risky, and you will not need to look for a temporary rental unit.

This important decision is an individual's own choice and depends upon the particular time and circumstances. Dealing with real estate may sometimes involve some risks, but for a substantial gain, you have to deal with these risks wisely, making your decisions intelligently and carefully. The possibility of profit-loss is present in any business decision. Therefore, in spite of all efforts to avoid risks, we should be ready for all outcomes. We have been blessed with this life, so as a grateful individual, we should acknowledge these blessings. If we face some risks or losses, we should show patience and contentment.

THE PROCEDURE OF SELLING A HOME

Our homes are great investments and are lifetime assets. If we need to sell our home for any reason, we should think twice, get full information and decide cautiously to take this large and sensitive step. In this regard, an important question arises in our minds: Should we sell it on our own or through a real estate agent? If you sell it yourself, you may save some money, but you have to understand it is not as simple as you may think. There is a lot of work, persistent effort and a complex system involved. You have to sacrifice a lot of time from your everyday life. In addition, a task like this requires hardship, labour and a lot of patience. You have to go through various stages of the selling process:

+ Home preparation
+ Conducting showings
+ Safety and security of your home and family
+ Dealing with buyers
+ Price negotiation
+ Completion of agreement
+ Getting the services of a lawyer

By handling the whole process yourself, you can save some money, but there are more chances of loss and inconvenience due to the lack of procedural knowledge to deal with every step. In addition, you can face many difficulties and complications in the process. If you use the services of a professional, it will be a lot easier to complete this transaction.

BENEFITS OF USING A REALTOR'S SERVICES

The selling process of a home is a complicated and lengthy one, which requires a great deal of patience. An experienced realtor will make this process easier by providing step-by-step guidance. An experienced professional can get you the highest possible price for your house. The following are some of the benefits of using the services of a professional real estate agent.

• PEACE OF MIND:

You will have peace of mind when you work with a realtor. These professionals adhere to a strict code of ethics, are insured and are committed to continuing education.

• BEST ADVICE:

Real estate agents have intimate knowledge of trends in the local marketplace, and so your realtor will be the best advisor throughout the transaction.

• FULL GUIDANCE FOR HOME PREPARATIONS:

When you work with a realtor, he or she will help you and provide tips to prepare your home for sale.

• HIGHEST PRICE ANALYSIS:

Your realtor will help you reach the highest possible price of your home.

- **EFFECTIVE MARKETING PLAN:**

On the basis of professional knowledge and training, your realtor will prepare the best marketing plan for your home to attain the highest possible value.

- **BEST NEGOTIATION METHODS:**

Your real estate agent is a qualified and trained negotiator and will negotiate on your behalf in the best manner, in order to protect you from complications and to get you the highest value for your home

- **CONNECTION WITH OTHER SERVICES:**

Your realtor will guide you and connect you with the best renovators, home stagers and lawyers.

COOPERATION AND CONFIDENCE IN YOUR REALTOR

A realtor is in fact a real estate "doctor" who plays an essential role in one of the most important matters of your life. He or she provides you the best advice and assistance in real estate matters. Think carefully about the choice you make; pick a realtor who is sincere, honest and experienced. Keep in mind the saying, "All that glitters is not gold."

Have a meeting with your chosen realtor at your home or office. In the beginning, decide the terms and conditions of your agreement, including the commission. That way no complications will be created later on. When you have agreed mutually, then you can rely on and have full confidence in your realtor, who is your business partner. When a strong and fully reliable relationship has been established, your realtor will use all of his or her capabilities and professionalism in dealing with your important matters.

IMPORTANT POINTS TO KEEP IN MIND WHEN SELLING YOUR HOUSE

• SELECTION OF A REALTOR:

If you have decided to use the services of a realtor, you should meet two to three realtors and have interviews with them. Ask them for references from their previous clients. Give priority to the best quality services, high performance and an impressive marketing plan. Also, negotiate matters of commission to determine the best choice for you.

• LISTING AGREEMENT:

There are two types of agreements being used in the real estate industry: open listing and exclusive listing.

1. Open Listing: Your house is advertised on Multiple Listing Service (MLS). The Toronto Real Estate Board (TREB) has the largest system in Canada, and approximately 38,000 realtors have access to this system. Due to open competition within the system, you have better chances to attain the highest value for your house.

2. Exclusive Listing: In this situation, your realtor can advertise and sell only through their brokerage. You can save some commission, but it will take a longer time to sell, and you are less likely to get the highest value.

Open listing on MLS is the best choice in order to sell faster and achieve the highest value.

PRICE EVALUATION OF YOUR HOUSE

A qualified and experienced real estate agent will suggest the market value of your home according to local market conditions, events, trends and recent sales of similar houses. You have full authority to fix the selling price. If you decide to put the selling price less than the market value, more buyers will take interest. That way there will be more chances to get multiple offers, and as a result, you can get the highest price and sell faster. On the other hand, if you list your home for a price that is higher than the market value, fewer buyers will be interested, and it will take longer to sell your house. The best policy is to adopt a moderate way in order to achieve the greatest results.

IMPORTANT THINGS TO DO BEFORE LISTING YOUR HOME

It is not a good idea to put your home in the market hastily and without adequate preparation. You should consult with your realtor before you offer your home for sale to prospective buyers. It is better to focus on the following important points:

• RENOVATION:

If you do some renovations to make your home more attractive, you can sell it faster and at a higher price. Give attention to overall condition as well as small details of your house, but specifically focus on the kitchen and washrooms. Fresh paint will give your home a new and refreshed look.

• START MOVING:

The more spacious your house is, the more attractive it will be to prospective buyers. Dispose of all unnecessary items from your home. You can pack them up in boxes and drop them off at donation centres.

• THOROUGH CLEANING:

Get your house cleaned thoroughly by a professional cleaning company to get the best results. Make your home spacious, airy and bright. When you have showings, clean and shine the floors again. Make it a routine for each showing.

• THE BEST FIRST IMPRESSION:

First impressions play an important role in the selling process. Give full attention to your home, and spend some money to upgrade the front area for a better look.

• PRE-INSPECTION:

If you get your home inspected before putting it up for sale, it will be much better for you. Ensure everything in your home is working properly; if it is not, it is advisable to fix it up. Then you will be satisfied, having full confidence and peace of mind during the sale of your house.

GOOD PLANNING TO SELL YOUR HOUSE

Consult with your realtor and ask him or her about their house-selling plans. Then you should cooperate with their plans and actions to sell your house faster and at the highest price. Some sellers do not give full cooperation to their realtors and therefore do not get the best possible results. Cooperating with a realtor in the following ways will help speed up the sale of your home: having a flexible schedule for home showings, not requiring a 24-hour notice, holding open houses and placing a "For Sale" sign at the front door.

The following are some very important points when selling your home:

- Advertisement on Multiple Listing Service (MLS)
- Internet advertising
- Sale sign at the front yard
- Conducting an open house
- Showings at short notice
- Long hours for showings
- Cooperation from tenants, if any
- Feedback from showings
- Effective communication
- Homeowner not present during showing
- Clear driveway during showing

TIPS TO GET THE BEST RESULTS

To reiterate, if you consider and act upon these important tips, you will be able to enjoy the best results.

- Pick and choose an honest, sincere and reliable realtor.
- Use reasonable and attractive sale prices.
- Decide faster if you are upgrading your home.
- Take your time if you are downsizing.
- Fix up the repair work first, and then sell.
- Make your home a showcase.
- Less is more—get rid of unnecessary items.
- Encourage and respect prospective buyers and agents.
- Always get a second opinion from the experts.
- Get a professional to take pictures and create a virtual video tour.
- Make your kitchen and washroom attractive.
- Make your house bright, fresh, airy and comfortable.
- Cooperate with bank appraisers and guide them for the improvement of your home.

+ Make your front entrance and front yard attractive to create a great first impression.
+ Focus on landscaping around your house.

QUICK REMINDERS FOR SHOWING YOUR HOME

+ Always remember the curb appeal.
+ De-clutter and show a spacious atmosphere.
+ Make your home anonymous and let the buyers imagine it as theirs.
+ A fresh coat of paint will make your house look like a model home.
+ Keep the home smelling fresh.
+ Make your house as bright as possible and let the sun shine in.
+ Minimum noise and light music is advisable.
+ Make all the washrooms spotless and gleaming.
+ Excuse yourself and your pets from your home during showings.

Good luck, homeowners! I hope you have immense success in selling your homes!

CHAPTER 10

WHAT IS THE FUTURE OF REAL ESTATE?

If we study and observe any country of the world, we will notice many of them have a lack of stability, a weak administration, poor economic conditions, lack of peace and safety, unrest and other various social deficiencies. Above all, there is often a lack of freedom in the expression of one's opinion. However, in the great country of Canada, we have a very distinct position in comparison. If you go to any corner of the world and ask the residents which country they think is best, Canada will definitely be among the top answers. They will show interest in living in Canada. International investors will be ready, without hesitation, to make an investment in Canada due to the following reasons:

REASONS FOR INVESTMENT IN CANADA

- Stable government: History shows that Canada has a comparatively strong and stable government. We have an effective administration system, an abundance of public welfare and benefits, and a great justice system. Thus, Canada is considered to be one of the best countries in which to live and invest.
- Effective Political Policies: If we study the past 25 years, we will see that Canada's political policies and strategies are very effective, successful and popular both domestically and

internationally. The Canadian people and the international community love and have respect for Canada and have full confidence that making an investment in this great country will prove to be fruitful.

- Underpopulated and vast in Size: Canada is massive in size but its population is quite low. Due to its attractive immigration policy and appealing education system, approximately 250,000 people from all parts of the world apply to move to Canada every year. They endeavour to make Canada their second home country, and this plays an important role in policies, economics and social and cultural lifestyles.

- Full Freedom and Peaceful Living: Immigrants who come to Canada from foreign countries to settle enjoy full freedom. They are free to reside in any province and start any legal business they like. They have opportunities for employment, enjoy all amenities of life and have freedom of conscience and freedom of expression. Every citizen's dignity and needs are looked after.

- Golden Opportunities of Investment: People from all over the world apply for immigration to Canada, as noted earlier. As a result, existing cities are expanding, and new suburban towns and cities are being built. There are many opportunities to start businesses to meet the needs of new immigrants in Canada.

- Stable and Safe Banking System: The banking system of Canada is quite effective, stable, safe and attractive. According to the Canadian Bankers Association (CBA), 87 percent of Canadians give banks a good performance rating when it comes to being secure and stable. The World Economic Forum has ranked the Canadian banking system as the most sound in the world for six years in a row. This strong and stable banking system of Canada is beneficial for all taxpayers, consumers, business owners and investors.

- <u>Canadian Health System</u>: The health care system in Canada is considered one of the best in the world, with its high standards and effectiveness. The government spends a substantial amount of money in the health sector to provide the best services to the public. Canadians enjoy some of the best medical treatment in the world.
- <u>Oil and Gas Industry</u>: Canada has been blessed with an abundance of resources like oil and gas. This great country is the sixth-largest oil producer in the world. In this sense, it is one of the most resource-rich countries in the world.
- <u>Mining Industry</u>: Canada is also blessed when it comes to the mining sector. It is abundant in minerals such as nickels, zinc and uranium.
- <u>Dividend Payments</u>: Canadian companies like banks, telecommunication companies, energy companies and others pay very high dividends to investors and shareholders. In this sense, they attract international investors on a large scale.
- <u>Friendly Atmosphere</u>: As mentioned earlier, Canada has a low population. The Canadian government offers immigration to qualified people all around the world every year. During the past 25 years, approximately 250,000 people have immigrated to Canada yearly and have settled freely. Canada has become a multicultural society, and settlers in Canada have great respect for each other. As a result, everybody enjoys a peaceful and friendly atmosphere.

BRIGHT FUTURE OF REAL ESTATE INVESTMENT

The investment of real estate is generally a very profitable business throughout the world. Canada has an especially unique position in regards to the real estate business sector. Real estate investment in Canada is very lucrative and can be considered a safe investment due to the following distinct features.

+ Canada is one of the most diplomatic countries in the world. It has established good relations with other countries and shows a loving character with the rest of the world. The government of Canada has attractive policies economically, politically and socially. It is like a safe haven for investment and living.

+ Canada is a country of peace. Its population consists of multicultural denominations. Its people are loving citizens. All of them enjoy a peaceful, friendly atmosphere, as well as freedom of speech and freedom of expression.

+ Canada is huge in size and is rather underpopulated. It has a vast geographical size and is full of natural resources. But because of the lack of population, these resources and treasures are not fully utilized. Thus, Canada is a land of opportunities to invest in many sectors.

+ Canada has an attractive immigration policy. The country welcomes many people for settlement, as mentioned earlier. Because approximately 250,000 people are settling in Canada every year, there is a high demand in the real estate sector.

+ Canada has a great banking system. Canada's banking system is very safe and established, and it offers high-quality services to consumers and investors. Canadian banks and other financial institutions have very attractive terms and conditions available for consumers, business owners and investors, especially for real estate needs and investments.

Considering the features mentioned above, investment of real estate in Canada is very safe, easy and attractive, and it can yield great dividends. No wise person can deny these favourable circumstances; rather, a wise person would be ready to invest in Canadian real estate without any hesitation.

VARIOUS TYPES OF INVESTMENT IN REAL ESTATE

The Residential Sector: This is the simplest kind of investment through which we can invest comfortably and confidently. It has minimal risk and has a high return on investment. It includes:

+ Single-family homes: The most profitable, because it is highly appreciative in value.
+ Low-rise buildings: Consist of duplex, triplex and fourplex. It is beneficial for small investors because it does not require substantial capital but still pays dividends.
+ High-rise buildings: Consist of rental apartment buildings, condos and towers. It requires a lot of capital and an effective management system.

Commercial Sector: This is a long-term business sector and generally suits above-average business people, with some exceptions. A sound and strong financial position is very important to have before investing and doing business in this sector. The following can be included in this sector:

+ Retail: Small units, private stores, chain stores, gas stations, grocery stores, hotels, restaurants.
+ Small plazas, strip malls, shopping centres, office buildings.
+ Large indoor and outdoor malls.

Industrial Sector: This is also a high-level investment. It can include the following:

+ Car wash, auto repair centre, storages.
+ Distribution centres, warehouses.
+ Manufacturing units, mills, factories.
+ Industrial unit development and construction.

The various sectors of investment mentioned above are important and profitable according to one's needs. The residential sector is the most common worldwide because a residence is one of the basic needs of life. Especially in Canada, the residential sector provides a simple and profitable investment opportunity. An individual consumer can buy a home with 5 percent down payment, get the benefit of an appealing rate of interest and enjoy profits with value appreciation.

Home buying and selling is a very profitable and safe investment. Commercial and industrial investments are also very profitable, but they require more capital to invest, and the interest rates are also higher than in the residential sector. Also, investors have to bear long-term obligations and responsibilities. One can do business in any of these sectors according to their abilities, interests and aptitudes.

RISKY TYPES OF INVESTMENT IN REAL ESTATE

Investment in real estate can be a sensitive decision. Investors must think thoroughly, plan properly and take proper steps when they are ready to invest. Some real estate properties generate only nominal profit and should be avoided in most cases. Here are some types of real estate investments to be cautious about:

+ Properties that do not generate rental income.
+ Properties with negative cash flow, i.e. Fancy condos, vacation rentals.
+ Tenant-in-common investment properties.
+ Development and deeds projects.
+ Condo hotels.
+ Time-share investment properties.
+ Foreign real estate investment.

THE BEST CANADIAN CITIES FOR REAL ESTATE INVESTMENT

According to the Real Estate Investment Network (REIN), investment of real estate in the following cities is likely to be the safest and most profitable when one considers local circumstances and future development projects.

+ Calgary, AB
+ Kitchener, Waterloo, ON
+ Edmonton, AB
+ Surrey, BC
+ Maple Ridge, BC
+ Hamilton, ON
+ St. Albert, AB
+ Simcoe County (Barrie, Orillia), ON
+ Red Deer, AB
+ Winnipeg, MB
+ Saskatoon, SK

FUTURE OF REAL ESTATE INVESTMENT

Real estate is flourishing and the value of properties is appreciating throughout the world, with some exceptions. Canada in particular has a very bright and promising future in all fields, especially in the real estate sector. The real estate sector is one of the pillars of the Canadian economic system. According to many economists, financial analysts and real estate experts, real estate in Canada provides us with safe, attractive and profitable investment opportunities.

I had the privilege of speaking with a long-time real estate expert and business and sales coach, Bruce Keith, on the topic of the "Future of Real Estate Investment." Mr. Keith, who has over 25 years of experience in the real estate industry, was kind enough to offer his words of advice regarding the future of real estate in Canada:

"The simplest way to evaluate the future of real estate in Canada is to look at the bigger picture. How is Canada viewed by the rest of the world? Typically Canada is perceived to be a beautiful country and a safe place to live. The population is made up of individuals who are healthy, easy to get along with, and always growing.

Look at that last statement…*healthy, easy to get along with, and always growing*. That's how you could view the future of real estate in Canada. Let's look at those three items individually:

Healthy – when the financial crash occurred in the United States in 2008 – 2009 the Canadian financial market (including real estate) was pretty much unaffected. House prices did not decline much if at all – nothing compared to what happened south of the border. Much of that can be attributed to the strength of our banking system and the lending regulations that have been in place for decades.

Easy to Get Along With – the Canadian real estate market is very predictable. There are never huge spikes in prices up or down. The market continues to rise predictably from year to year. Of course, there are periodic "bumps in the road" but they typically are minor and do not last long.

Always Growing – there are two components to this observation. One is the steady increase in the population and another is the fact that prices continue to rise all across the country. As a relative as a result of those two components, real estate as an investment is very dependable in Canada. Very few surprises and because the economy is so strong, the growth in housing value mirrors that."

These sentiments offered by Mr. Keith have distinctly stood out in my mind. I attended the annual conference "Realtor Quest" on May 6 and 7, 2015. This event is Canada's largest trade show and conference for realtors; it is organized by the Toronto Real Estate Board (TREB).

Many great speakers, presenters and experts in the real estate and financial industry shared their insightful knowledge with realtors at this conference. I had the opportunity to attend excellent presentations led by the likes of Bruce Keith, Jason Mercer, Don Patterson and Warren Jestin.

My own personal experience in the industry and the great insight provided by these accomplished experts have led me to conclude that, without a doubt, Canada is a great country and is a land of opportunities. It has a bright and prosperous future and I see Canada as a shining star!

We should capitalize on the opportunities given to us in Canada. Anyone who is interested in investing and taking advantage of these golden opportunities can prosper and make their dreams come true!

Dear readers! Thank you for taking the time to read this book. I hope and pray that my humble efforts in writing this book prove to be beneficial and useful for you in your future endeavours and in fulfilling your dreams and goals. Always remember, the sky is the limit!

Printed in the United States
By Bookmasters